STA...

OLD STYLE

CONJURE

WISDOMS, WORKINGS AND REMEDIES

Starr Casas

Old Style Conjure

Wisdoms, Workings and Remedies

Pendraig
Publishing
Los Angeles, CA 91040

Old Style Conjure
Wisdoms, Workings and Remedies
by Starr Casas
First Edition © 2014
by PENDRAIG Publishing
All rights reserved.

Cover Design,
Interior Images,   Jo-Ann Byers Mierzwicki
Typeset & Layout

PENDRAIG Publishing
Los Angeles, CA 91040
www.PendraigPublishing.com
Printed in the United States of America

ISBN: 978-1-936922-73-4

WARNING!

Any reader who uses the work
within this book
does so entirely at their own risk.

The author and publisher accept no liability
if the work does not have the desired effect

or

if adverse effects are caused.

This book is not suitable for children.

DEDICATION

I dedicate this book
to all the folks who walk beside me
in my life on-line
and in my world.

I thank you all!

TABLE OF CONTENTS

INTRODUCTION

After many requests for my daily wisdom's that I post on my Facebook page to be turned into a book I decided to write this little book on "Conjure Wisdoms, Workings and Remedies". I'm a firm believer that we are what we claim. We have to all remember that we are what we think of ourselves. If you think you have nothing and that you are worth nothing then that is what you are calling to your spirit. I learned a long time ago to watch how I think of myself; because it is easy to think down on ones-self and it can become a habit quickly.

You have to remember that you cannot please all the people all of the time. Some folks you can't please at all no matter what you do or no matter how you try to bend over backwards to try and be what they want you to be. Once you fall into that trap it's very hard to get out of. The only person that you have to please is yourself. If folks are finding things wrong with you and things you need to change then you need to put them to kicking rocks.

I have found that this is a way to control a person. I know that some parents are very critical of their children and then these children grow up to be adults what they've heard their whole lives they begin to believe. I was lucky and instead of my Mama tearing us down she built us up. I'm a firm believer that no one is more important than I also that no one can validate me or love me like I love myself. This is the lesson my Mama taught us as we were growing up as children.

I understand that some folks weren't that lucky but I'm here to tell you now you should always love yourself. When folks start pointing out issues with other folks then this tells me that they are insecure and they need that to make them feel better about themselves. I think that everyone should have the right to say how they feel to be able to be themselves and to be able to be all that they can be and hold their spirits up high; without someone coming along and telling them all about themselves.

As a worker of over 40 years I have seen all kinds of folks with low self-esteem. They have come through all walks of life and it's always the same thing and sometimes the stories are so similar that you would think you were talking to the same client over and over again. I'm here to tell you right now that nobody and I mean nobody has the right to make you feel that you are less than you really are. Someone once said that in order to do this work or to give advice on the situation that you have to have walked in that person's shoes. Well I've had those shoes on my feet and I've had to work hard to pull them off.

I used the trick that my Mama taught us as children to build up our self-esteem. When I was in my early 20s I stood in front of the mirror a many of nights talking to my spirit and look into my own eyes in that mirror. In order for a person to be or to become all that they should be or want to be in their lives they have to love themselves. I'm not talking about being selfish and thinking that your all that in a bag of chips and you're the best in the world; I'm talking about seeing yourself for the beautiful, strong, caring person you are.

You cannot let anyone make you feel that you are less than you are no matter who they are. Nobody in this life is perfect but we all have the right to make our dreams come true. We all have the right to love ourselves and to think that we are special and unique in our own way. That we offer something to the world and to the folks around us that no one else can offer because there is only one of each of us. The only way that I know to change the way you think about yourself is to speak directly to your spirit. If you practice this daily your spirit is going to become strong and will believe the words you are saying. No one can hold you back but you!

If you bought this book I would like to think that you're ready to help yourself to be happy, prosperous and successful in your life. This is not something that someone can do for you this is something that you have to do for yourself. Don't worry about what folks have told you about yourself; KNOW that you deserve everything that you want and everything that you need in your life. So make up your mind to do a good strong cleansing and to start out changin' the way you think about yourself. Instead of focusing on what's wrong with you, focus on what's right. I'm goin' to give a little exercise that I've used in the pas,t I haven't used it in a long time because I have not needed it. If you do this every day you should see great results in no time at all.

This works for just about any issue that you have, of course nothing is guaranteed in this life and nothing comes easy when you're dealing with your spirit and your life. I stopped smoking doing this. I was smoking almost 5 packs of cigarettes a day. Who would've thought telling myself that I didn't smoke and that I didn't like smoking as I was smoking a cigarette would have helped me stop smoking? It's the truth! Every time I'd light a cigarette I'd say I don't smoke anymore but I don't mind if other folks smoke. I never wanted to be one of those folks who stopped smoking and complained about everybody else that smoked. If I could stop smoking this away then you can make the changes within your spirit that you need too.

The key to this is sticking with it don't just work at it a few days and then stop. Keep at it even when it seems like it's doing no good. What I want you to do is every night before you go to bed after you've had your bath. Stand in front of the bathroom mirror or any mirror and say "nobody loves me like I love me"! Repeat it at least three times then go to bed. Follow up with this book; say one saying daily throughout the whole day. It takes a while to change our thoughts so just keep at it and after a while you won't even have to think about it, you will KNOW you are all that!

The next step to this is to do a little spiritual work on you. I suggest that you take a white candle and you brush yourself off with the candle going downward from head to toe and then pushing outward; don't dress this candle. Really focus on your head. Light the candle and let it burn for about 15 minutes then put the candle out. The next day repeat the process; continue with this until the candle is totally burned down.

This is the last step get you a pen and a pad. Draw the line down the center of the paper. On one side write down all your good qualities and on the other side write down the things you want to change about yourself. Once you're finished tear the page in half; burn the side that has the qualities you want to change about yourself. Then take the ashes outside then blow them to the West; if you don't have a West then just blow them away from you.

The next day after you start your candle sit down and repeat this process. The goal of this process is to end up with a blank side of the paper that represents the qualities you want to change about yourself. I don't have a PhD nor am I a Dr., but I know from experience that these things can help you if you follow the instructions. Any time that we don't feel or think that we're good enough or feel or think that we can't do anything, we are holding ourselves back. We all have a right to be able to live our lives in peace and harmony happiness and prosperity. In order to do this we have to think very highly of ourselves.

It is my hope that this book will help those who read it in some small way. I truly know what it is to me your spirit up lifted. I am a walking testament that these steps work; all you have to do is stick with it. You also have to know that you deserve everything you want in your life. All you have to do is claim it.

Days of the Week

From the
Old Style Conjure Candle Burning Book

Before anyone starts talking out of the side of their mouth, this list of the days of the week can also be found in my "Candle Burning Book". I'm adding it here because not everyone has the "Candle Burning Book" but we also need the list of colors for the daily candle burning.

Monday — is associated with the Moon
    Candle colors — white or gray
        Crossroads work to learn to read cards, dealing with family matters, Protection, Truth, Peace, Justice

Tuesday — is associated with Mars
    Candle colors — Red or Orange
    Taking Action, Crossing, Uncrossing work,

Aggression, Cut & Clear work, Law Stay Away, All Battles

Wednesday — is associated with Mercury
    Candle colors — Purple
        Mastery, Domination Work, Wisdom, Healing, Dealing with Legal problems.

Thursday — is associated with Jupiter
    Candle colors — Green, Purple, Orange, or Blue
        Business, Gambling, Power, Material Wealth, Luck, Road Opening

Friday — is associated with Venus
    Candle colors — Green, Red, Blue, White, Purple
        Love, Marriage, Money, Attraction, Luck, Healing, Prosperity, Change, Road Opening work, Bring Peace, Relationships, Power and Success

Saturday — is associated with Saturn
    Candle colors — Black, Grey, and White
        Binding, Obstacles, Justice, Reversal, Uncrossing, Crossing, Cut and Clear work

Sunday — is associated with the Sun
    Candle colors — Red, Gold, and Orange
        This is a Leo's power day, Power, Health, Success, Personal Finances, Prosperity, Home life, Control, Hotfoot work, Shut your mouth conjure, Sunday is good for all hot work.

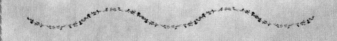

Month of January

Trivia: In the ole days folks thought garnets had powers because of their red color; it was thought they could offer protection from bleeding.

Herb of the Month: Rue
Candle Color: Blue or Green
First Holy Stone: Jasper
Birthstone Pendulum: Garnet

Day 1:

I walk into the NEW YEAR with my head held high and Prosperity, Love, Honor and Success as my Companions!

Day 2:

Anything is possible with prayer, faith and Conjure work!

Day 3

Are you ready to shine? Pray in the light at sun rise!

Day 4

Let the power of prayer and the flame of a candle draw what you need!

Day 5

When I believe in myself ALL things are possible!

Day 6

I choose to allow wonderful things and PROSPERITY to flow into my life.

Day 7

When you are loaded with troubles and need to put them to rest; do a cleansing and bury it in the West!

Day 8

I am a magnet! I draw positive things into my life!

Day 9

When one door to happiness closes, another WILL open, don't take too long at the closed door or you'll miss the opened one!

Day 10

We all need the flame of a candle to light our way sometimes!

Day 11

I open the roads to love, joy, freedom, and I open my heart to wisdom!

Day 12

I am a magnet of TOTAL success name it and claim it!

Day 13

We are what we think, plant the seed the tree to prosperity will grow!

Day 14

Does it seem like a mountain is in your way? Call on the power of Moses to move it!

Day 15

I have the ability to conquer all challenges; my success is a GIVEN.

Day 16

My life is built on a road that can only go toward success happiness, fulfillment, love and prosperity.

Day 17

Money is mine I name it, I claim it, I KNOW it, I draw it into my hands!

Day 18

My life is built on a strong foundation; I choose my own road to success and wisdom.

Day 19

We are what we think, cut and clear the negative out of your thinking!

Day 20

When wisdom seems to be out of reach, carry a pinch of Solomon Seal root!

Day 21

I release all my fears, worries and drama that drain my spirit daily.

Day 22

Work the root and draw JUSTICE on your side!

Day 23

To accomplish your goals give them to your God for him to hold!

Day 24

I acknowledge my confidence, my knowledge, my self-worth; my spirit is soaring towards greatness.

Day 25

I glow and radiate with success, happiness, and prosperity in my life on all levels!

Day 26

Cut the ties that bind you, set your spirit free to find happiness and TOTAL success!

Day 27

I take full responsibility for everything I do in my life! Total success follows me with every step I take!

Day 28

When we fail we are one step closer to Success!

Day 29

Do you have walls blocking your every move? Pray Joshua 6 and let God tear down those walls as he did the walls of Jericho.

Day 30

    If you blow upon a spark, it quickens into flame, if you spit on it, it dies out; yet both you do with your mouth!

Day 31

    A blow from a whip raises a welt, but a blow from the tongue smashes bones!

MONTH OF FEBRUARY

Trivia: In the year of 1999 there wasn't a full moon. This is the only time this has happen in recorded history.

Herb of the Month: Violet
Candle Color: Blue or Purple
Second Holy Stone: Sapphire
Birthstone Pendulum: Amethyst

Day 1

My Ancestor's guide and protect me with every step I take in my life.

Day 2

You can let your day come and go or face it with love, joy and success.

Day 3

As you seal up your silver and gold, so balance and weigh your words.

Day 4

Take care not to slip by your tongue and fall victim to your foe waiting in ambush.

Day 5

I am healthy wealthy and wise I accept my success, prosperity and long life!

Day 6

I control my life; I create my world my success and my happiness. My world is MINE!

Day 7

Don't focus on what you don't have; give thanks for what you do have then CLAIM what you want!

Day 8

Today I look at myself with approval I am worthy of love honor and glory!

Day 9

Success is my right hand man where I go he follows!

Day 10

I am healthy wealthy and wise! I radiate success, prosperity, happiness in a drama free life!

Day 11

I judge myself with love, honor and respect, for I am all I want to be!

Day 12

Forever I march forward crowned in triumph, victorious with success!

Day 13

I am deeply rooted with a firm hold on my happiness. NOTHING can derail me from my goal!

Day 14

I praise myself daily even for my flaws; they are just rough edges that will smooth over time!

Day 15

I open my arms to the flow and the rhyme of my success; I embrace my heart's desire!

Day 16

My friends do not judge me, nor do they influence what I do with my life.

Day 17

No matter which road life takes me down I find power, wisdom, self-worth with an abundance of love and joy!

Day 18

Conjure work can open the door to Attraction!

Day 19

Be like the little red train; don't think you can KNOW you can!

Day 20

Have you lost your way and you don't know which fork in the road to take? Let me throw the bones for you!

Day 21

All the branches on my tree flourish; they are deep rooted in love compassion and success!

Day 22

No violent winds can uproot my tree; nor can envy, jealousy, nor hate harm me! My enemies are speechless and prostrate!

Day 23

My life is assured great confront, love, happiness and success. All great things are mine for the asking!

Day 24

All of life's problems pass over me like a shadow and like a fleeting rumor, for nothing binds my spirit!

Day 25

You can let your day come and go or face it with love, joy and success.

Day 26

Today I release the past, so I can grow into my future!

Day 27

I judge myself with love, honor and respect, for I am all I want to be!

Day 28

Forever I march forward crowned in triumph, victorious with success!

MONTH OF MARCH

Trivia: In Roman times March was the beginning of the year. It was the very first month.

Herb of the Month: Daffodil
Candle Color: Green
Third Holy Stone: Chalcedony
Birthstone Pendulum: Aquamarine

Day 1

All gossip, envy and jealousy moves away from me like smoke scattered by the wind, it just fades away!

Day 2

I have received a splendid crown from my God; I am crowned with love, honor and success!

Day 3

I am in authority of my own life; I trust my own judgment, wisdom, and knowledge I sit in my own counsel.

Day 4

Take care not to slip by your tongue and fall victim to your foe waiting in ambush.

Day 5

Don't focus on what you don't have give thanks for what you do have and CLAIM what you want!

Day 6

I am healthy wealthy and wise! I radiate success, prosperity, happiness in a drama free life!

Day 7

No matter which road life takes me down I find power, wisdom, self-worth with an abundance of love and Success.

Day 8

I am deeply rooted with a firm hold on my happiness. NOTHING can derail me from my goal!

Day 9

My life is assured great confront, love, happiness and success. All great things are mine for the asking!

Day 10

I open my arms to the flow and the rhyme of my success; I embrace my heart's desire!

Day 11

I have received a splendid crown from my God; I am crowned with love, honor and success!

Day 12

If you have the blues then light a blue candle dressed with Old Style Conjure clarity oil and find the light at the end of the tunnel!

Day 13

Today I release the past, so I can grow into my future!

Day 14

You are a magnet of TOTAL success name it and claim it!

Day 15

I praise myself daily even for my flaws; they are just rough edges that will smooth over time!

Day 16

All the branches on my tree flourish; they are deep rooted in love compassion and success!

Day 17

We are what we think, plant the seed the tree to prosperity will grow!

Day 18

As you seal up your silver and gold, so balance and weigh your words

Day 19

Today I look at myself with approval. I am worthy of love honor and glory!

Day 20

I am healthy, wealthy and wise. I accept my success, prosperity and long life!

Day 21

When wisdom seems to be out of reach, carry a pinch of Solomon Seal root!

Day 22

Today I accept and acknowledge all the gifts MY God has blessed me with and I walk in faith!

Day 23

Success follows me every step I take, I move forward into my dreams!

Day 24

I claim all that I want and all that I need; today the road is paved with prosperity, happiness, and love!

Day 25

Success is MINE! I claim it and name it!

Day 26

Today I conquer all challenges and those who would hold me back! I will either step over them, around them or through them!

Day 27

I have my feet planted on a firm foundation;

there is no strong wind that can move me unless it is to help me move forward!

Day 28

All blocks and crossed conditions fall like dust under my feet; I am wise and empowered by my God!

Day 29

I share my Joy and Love with all I come in contact with today!

Day 30

Today I honor those who have paved the way for me.

Day 31

Today I vow to myself, I will Love, Honor, and Rejoice in my being! My LIGHT Shines!

MONTH OF APRIL

Trivia: April is from the Roman word Aprilis which is derived from aperio, aperire, apertus, a verb meaning "to open". The Fasti Praenestini offered the expanded explanation that "fruits and flowers and animals and seas and lands do open."

Herb of the Month:	Sweet Pea
Candle Color:	White or Yellow
Fourth Holy Stone:	Emerald
Birthstone Pendulum:	Diamond

Day 1

I refuse to let my fears of success hold me back, today I cut those binds and set my spirit free, so I can be all I want to be!

Day 2

> May those who try to hold me back be like smoke on a windy day! POOF they're GONE!

Day 3

> I remove the blinders of fear and regret! I see clearly now which road to travel!

Day 4

> ALL obstacles are removed out of my way! I move forward towards my goals.

Day 5

> When life throws you a lemon sweeten it with a little Rootwork!

Day 6

> I pray that MY God will give me the strength to stay true to myself and those around me!

Day 7

> Today even with the storm of haters raging around me I KNOW I am loved and protected!

Day 8

> Today I am stress free, my trouble are washed away like a cleansing rain!

Day 9

> Every action causes a reaction Today I choose to think calmly before I react!

Day 10

> I am thankful today for everything I have! I KNOW the rest will come; I'm crowned with success!

Day 11

Money comes, Money goes, Money stays, Money Flows, Money is MINE for me to hold!

Day 12

Today I stand firm against the ongoing vices of my haters! The more they push the stronger my stance will become UNMOVEABLE!

Day 13

Today I am marking the road to my success! I am empowered by My God and the folks who walk with me in my world!

Day 14

Prosperity flows into my household! Today I walk in peace and gratitude!

Day 15

There is only today and TODAY I walk in Love, Honor and SUCCESS!

Day 16

Today I choose to look forward to the future because yesterday is gone!

Day 17

I am thankful for all the folks that walk beside me, plus the haters because they make me appreciate the folks who stand beside me all the more!

Day 18

I am thankful for I have been blessed with and for all the blessings to come!

Day 19

Today I choose to get up off my butt and work towards what's mine!

Day 20

I am thankful for all that is mine and all that will be mine! There is no end to MY dreams!

Day 21

Today I keep moving forward and I refuse to get side tracked from my goals!

Day 22

I am crowned in success and victorious in all my battles even if they are up hill!

Day 23

I choose to make my life what I want it to be NOT how others think it should be!

Day 24

Lord today I pray you give me the strength to stay true to myself and those around me!

Day 25

Today I continue forward towards my goals no matter how far and out of reach they may seem!

Day 26

Today I'm off my butt and on my feet moving at a good pace towards my dreams!

Day 27

The only approval I need is my OWN and today my spirit approves of every step I take towards my goals!

Day 28

Why reach for the stars when you can have the whole universe, start reaching for those dreams!

Day 29

Today I look at folks with a clear vision to see what is really hidden in their heart; ALL confusion is REMOVED from my world!

Day 30

Yesterday is GONE and tomorrow never comes so get out of the past and start moving towards your goals!

MONTH OF MAY

Trivia: May was named after the Greek goddess Maia, who was identified with the Roman era goddess of fertility, Bona Dea, whose festival was held in May.

Herb of the Month:	Daisy
Candle Color:	Green
Fifth Holy Stone:	Sardonyx
Birthstone Pendulum:	Emerald

Day 1

> *Today I flush the words "I Can't" I can and I WILL achieve all my goals and my dreams!*

Day 2

There is no future, there is NO past, there is only today and TODAY I walk in Love, Honor and SUCCESS!

Day 3

With every stall there is a fresh start, don't let the stall's in life sidetrack you from your goal!

Day 4

I finish this day knowing that tomorrow will be a better day and I'm one step closer to my dreams!

Day 5

Today I honor those who have gone before me; who guide me on my road to happiness and success.

Day 6

Success is a frame of mind today I set my spirit in the right frame!

Day 7

My success is a straight shot, with curves and shit in it that lead to my goals of love happiness and prosperity!

Day 8

Today I take the first step forward to letting my little light shine; I'm moving toward success!

Day 9

Even when the storms are brewing, I KNOW the bright like of the Sun will drive them away!

Day 10

Today I walk in Victory towards my success! I KNOW my God's Blessings rain down on my head!

Day 11

I am grateful today for all my blessings even if I didn't realize at the time they were blessings!

Day 12

I make my own destination and today this train is headed towards Success, Love and Happiness!

Day 13

Today I release all fear and I walk towards my dreams instead of away from them.

Day 14

I accept every NEW opportunity that comes my way that flows with my spirit!

Day 15

Today I stop WISHING for my dreams to come true! I'm gonna MAKE them happen!

Day 16

Today I shake off the fear that is holding me back; I open my heart mind and spirit to my success!

Day 17

Even when I stumble I refuse to fall, I will continue on my way to my destination of wisdom, prosperity and success!

Day 18

All challenges are moved out of my way, the road to success is smooth.

Day 19

Doubtfulness has no place in my world; I know what direction I am going in! The direction of SUCCESS!

Day 20

Every day that you lounge around your dreams are passing you by; Get up grab your dreams and MAKE them happen!

Day 21

All things that are hidden will come to light, I choose to sit back and wait!

Day 22

I accept everything that comes my way today, even when I have to work towards success!

Day 23

I CLAIM Victory over those who think they are more deserving than I am; or who thinks they run shit!

Day 24

I follow my own tune, which will lead me to happiness, prosperity, and success!

Day 25

The foundation of my life is built on success happiness, fulfillment, love and prosperity.

Day 26

> Today I choose to fight the current because I refuse to just go with the flow!

Day 27

> I know for every storm that brews the sun will shine and peace will flow through like a fresh cool breeze!

Day 28

> New opportunities are around every corner; all I have to do is open my arms and KNOW I deserve them.

Day 29

> Today I take the time to pluck the thorns that block my path! I'm clearing the way for prosperity, love and success!

Day 30

> Today I acknowledge my achievements, my successes, my goals and the pride I feel within my spirit to have the strength to KNOW my worth!

Day 31

> Today I refuse to let challenges stand in my way! I sweep them out like sweeping dirt out the door!

MONTH OF JUNE

Trivia: Queen Elizabeth II was crowned Queen of Great Britain in the Month of June.

Herb of the Month:	Honey Suckle
Candle Color:	Yellow
Sixth Holy Stone:	Carnelian
Birthstone Pendulum:	Pearls

Day 1

When one door closes another door opens! Today I walk through the door to love, honor, happiness and SUCCESS!

Day 2

This morning I give thanks for everything I have and everything I will have!

Day 3

Today I refuse to let my faith be dimmed by fear; I move forward and I claim a strong faith where there is NO room for doubt!

Day 4

I realize today that whatever I see for myself is what I am drawing and claiming in my life!

Day 5

Today I choose to SWEEP around my own door stoop and let others clean up their own messes!

Day 6

I follow my own dreams, I don't have time to worry about what my neighbor is dreaming, and I'm too busy claiming my own!

Day 7

With every step I take into my future I choose to leave the past and all its baggage behind!

Day 8

Today I refuse to let someone else's issues become mine! The weight of the world floats off my shoulders and into the open space.

Day 9

Why walk? Today I choose to ride on the power of success, happiness and prosperity!

Day 10

Today I remove those things that are a weight around my neck; if I can't change them I choose to cut them free!

Day 11

It's not who you are that keeps you from success; it's the limitation you set on yourself that stops you!

Day 12

I refuse to sit around and wait for my life too happen; I intend to move forward and MAKE things happen!

Day 13

My faith is strong! I know that over every hill I have to cross there is a green valley waiting for me.

Day 14

Today I pick and choose the things I keep in my life; the rest I set free on the winds to be swept away!

Day 15

I am the master of my life; No mountain can stand in my way! Forever I march forward crowned in success!

Day 16

I choose not to wait for success to find me; I'm set on the road to finding it!

Day 17

Today I am thankful for my Ancestors; I choose to walk on a road that will honor them!

Day 18

Today I CLAIM Victory over those who would hold me back and try to make me feel less than I am!

Day 19

I flow through the garden that is my life; I accept the fruits of my labor with open arms and a joyous heart!

Day 20

Today I choose to let go of the old to make room for the new successful prosperous ME!

Day 21

Today I choose to open my arms and accept all opportunities to increase my income given by my God!

Day 22

Today I let the healing power of my God wash over me, cleanse me and I draw in all that is mine!

Day 23

I accept all the great things that are mine! Success, prosperity, love, joy and happiness!

Day 24

I acknowledge that what I claim is mine! Today I claim my heart's desire!

Day 25

Today I choose to approve of myself; my flaws are just stepping stones on the road to perfection!

Day 26

I am deeply rooted with a firm hold on my life! I am powerful within my spirit and I walk the road to success!

Day 27

All my troubles and worries fall away like the leaves in autumn to make room for love happiness and joy!

Day 28

Even when the storms of life blow through I choose to believe they are blowing out what I don't need any more!

Day 29

All gossip, envy and jealousy moves away from me; I refuse to let it invade my world.

Day 30

Even when the odds are against me I see success at the end of the tunnel!

MONTH OF JULY

Trivia: July is the Month of Parent's Day.

Herb of the Month: Water Lily
Candle Color: Red
Seventh Holy Stone: Chrysolite
Birthstone Pendulum: Ruby

Day 1

I choose to walk with a strong faith; I know that everything I need will be provided!

Day 2

Today I choose to STOP letting folks get in my way, I control my life, my success and my happiness! Haters move aside!

Day 3

I refuse to let my enemies knock me down, the harder they try the harder I'll fight to stay standing on firm ground!

Day 4

I refuse to walk in someone else shadow, I prefer to let my own light shine and walk toward success!

Day 5

Who you are doesn't hold you back, it's who and what you think you're not that holds you back!

Day 6

Forever I march forward crowned in success, victorious with triumph! I have all I want and all I need!

Day 7

I refuse to be led down someone else road! Today I choose to follow my own road to my own dreams!

Day 8

I choose to let go of all the aches and pains, within my body only a healthy spirit rules!

Day 9

We are what we think! I choose to think that I am well loved, honored, and very successful!

Day 10

I choose to watch what folks do; instead of what they say! Actions always speak louder than words!

Day 11

Get motivated and start taking the steps toward your goal; leave the talking to others.

Day 12

I may not know it all but I know without a doubt I am blessed and walk on the path to success!

Day 13

You can't turn back time, but today I choose to start a new time with a new outcome one that is filled with joy, and self-love.

Day 14

Nothing will happen as long as I sit still; today I choose to get things moving around on the road to love, success and prosperity.

Day 15

Today I choose to STOP holding onto my unworthiness, and open the door to success, power and love. I am worthy of ALL I want!

Day 16

I am powerful! Today I stop letting folks make me feel unworthy. I break free of the BINDS they have put on me!

Day 17

If you have no enemy within eating at you, then the enemies on the outside can't touch you!

Day 18

It doesn't matter what your critics have to say. There has never been a critic honored they are pushed into the dark!

Day 19

My life is what I choose to make it and I choose to make it joyful, loving, prosperous and successful!

Day 20

Today I choose to walk through the door of joy, love, and success!

Day 21

Every achievement starts with a goal, and every goal begins with a dream, I achieve my dreams one step at the time towards success!

Day 22

Today even my flaws shine like the brightest star in the sky; they are just my spirit shifting in the RIGHT direction!

Day 23

I control my own success, my own destiny, and my world; NO one can stop this train from rolling! Move over cause I'm coming through!

Day 24

I claim success, joy, peace and happiness! My world revolves around what I claim!

Day 25

My spirit is so light that I float through life on a cloud of, love, success, power and prosperity. There's no rain in my cloud!

Day 26

No mountain can stand in my way! My spirit will either go over it, under it, around it or through it to find my success!

Day 27

Whatever I claim in my world belongs to me. Today I claim and abundance of love, prosperity and joy!

Day 28

When one door closes another will open, today I choose to follow spirit and walk through the RIGHT door!

Day 29

My inner light shines so bright that the darkness fears it! Only blessings are welcome in my world!

Day 30

Every thought causes an action and every action causes a reaction; I am ever mindful of my action!

Day 31

I know myself worth I have a healthy ego that draws success and prosperity into my life.

MONTH OF AUGUST

Trivia: August is the month of the Lion. The month was originally named Sextilis which means six in Latin.

Herb of the Month:	Jezebel Root
Candle Color:	Orange
Seventh Holy Stone:	Beryl
Birthstone Pendulum:	Peridot

Day 1

I am the master of my life; I decide what enters into my realm!

Day 2

When your enemies are breathing down your neck then you KNOW you are moving in the right direction!

Day 3

I pray daily for the spirit of wisdom to walk beside; so I always know which fork in the road to take because wisdom leads to greatness!

Day 4

Today I will be silent and listen when others speak; I will listen with an open heart and mind!

Day 5

God of my ancestors give me the strength to let go of all things that are holding me back! I claim VICTORY!

Day 6

I am the navigator of my own destiny; I follow the path to good health, love, honor, success and prosperity!

Day 7

I have no right to criticize myself but I have every right to praise, love and be joyful with myself.

Day 8

Have you lost your way and you don't know which fork in the road to take? Call on the power of Wisdom to find your way!

Day 9

I am unhampered, because I have the firm, secure, tranquil, all-powerful, all-seeing, spirit of my God that walks with me!

Day 10
>
> I make only the right choices for me, I trust my intuition to guide me, and I trust my decisions.

Day 11

> I love, honor and approve of myself, I hold myself up high with the power my God has given me.

Day 12

> I choose to find hope where I can't see any, I choose to stand strong against all opposition, and I am an unmovable POWER!

Day 13

> Today I make the right choices; I have the wisdom and knowledge to make smart decisions today. I am on the right path!

Day 14

> I solve all issues and challenges that come my way today with wisdom, insight, and love.

Day 15

> I am healthy, wealthy and wise! I walk in the light of enlightenment with every step I take!

Day 16

> I let my fears, I radiate with success, happiness, and prosperity in my life!

Day 17

> Don't focus on what you don't have; give thanks for what you do have and CLAIM what you want!

Day 18

I take full responsibility for everything I do in my life! Total success follows me with every step I take!

Day 19

Today I cut the ties that bind me; I set my spirit free to find happiness and TOTAL success!

Day 20

Air upon a spark, quickens into flame, if you spit on it, it dies out; yet you do them both with your mouth!

Day 21

Don't slip by your tongue and fall victim to your foe waiting in ambush for you.

Day 22

Watch, look and listen more to a foes action more than their words!

Day 23

Today I release the past, so I can grow into my future! I move forward into my own personal power.

Day 24

A blow from the whip leaves strips, but a blow from the tongue destroys spirits!

Day 25

I let go of past hurts and feeling of being unwanted I open my arms wide to fill that void with love!

Day 26

Today I walk in the light of my own success!

Day 27

Today I let go of what I can't change and move forward to the things I can.

Day 28

I refuse to let my fears, worries and other's drama drain my spirit, and I stand on a strong firm foundation!

Day 29

I glow and radiate with success, happiness, and prosperity in my life on all levels!

Day 30

My Ancestor's guide and protect me with every step I take in my life.

Day 31

I am healthy wealthy and wise I accept my success, prosperity and long life!

MONTH OF SEPTEMBER

Trivia: September is the month of the harvest moon.

Herb of the Month: Morning Glory
Candle Color: White
Seventh Holy Stone: Topaz
Birthstone Pendulum: Sapphire

Day 1
  Today I refuse to let self-pity enter my thoughts! I am loved, honored and cherished!

Day 2
  Today I let go of all self-pity; it blows away like smoke on the wind!

Day 3

I love, honor and approve of myself; self-pity is out the door!

Day 4

Today I trust myself to make the right choices for my life; I'm building a strong foundation.

Day 5

I have a strong inner strength that can't be destroyed!

Day 6

Today I am strong in the knowledge that I love myself!

Day 7

Today the smoke of confusion fades away and I see what is before me! SUCCESS!

Day 8

I choose my friends who honor me as I honor them with love.

Day 9

Today I cut all ties with jealousy, envy and turmoil! My life is going in a positive direction.

Day 10

I let go of all self-pity and turmoil my life is built on love I am cherished.

Day 11

All of my roads lead to prosperity, love, success and happiness!

Day 12

Today all of my haters are gone like smoke on the wind!

Day 13

Every mountain I climbed a green Valley full of abundance and happiness waits for me.

Day 14

Today I let go of all the hurt and turmoil that I've been holding onto. I set myself free!

Day 15

Today I cut and clear those who judge me and hurt me out of my life! I am loved and honored!

Day 16

I am beautiful, smart, courageous, prosperous, and successful! Today I claim my dreams.

Day 17

I embrace myself with love and joy, today I move forward to a glorious life!

Day 18

I refuse to be a victim of my fear and worries; today I cut them loose and set myself free.

Day 19

For every door that closes two more will open I choose to walk through the door of self-love, prosperity and success!

Day 20

Today I claim my personal power; I can solve any problem that comes my way with success!

Day 21

Today I refuse to let doubt and worry enter into my thoughts. I can handle any situation that comes along.

Day 22

I approve of myself with love; I know I am a shining bright star!

Day 23

I walk in the Valley of milk and honey my life is a blessing!

Day 24

Today I decide to cut the past free and move forward in my life.

Day 25

Today I tear down all the walls that have been built around me! I live my life by my standards!

Day 26

Today I refuse to let others judgments of me affect my life; I'm the only one who can judge me!

Day 27

The judgments of others on my life are being cut and cleared today!

Day 28

My life is filled with love and happiness; everything I won't or need is provided!

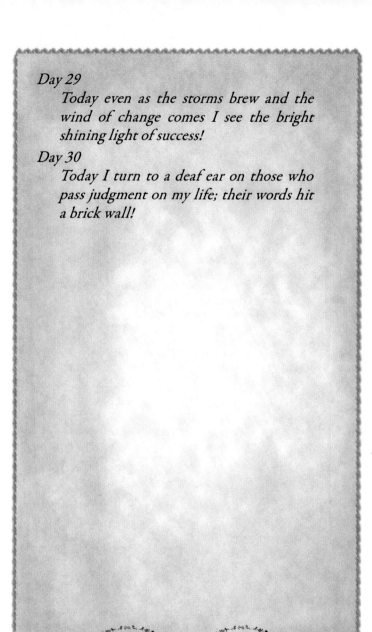

Day 29

Today even as the storms brew and the wind of change comes I see the bright shining light of success!

Day 30

Today I turn to a deaf ear on those who pass judgment on my life; their words hit a brick wall!

Month of October

Trivia: October retained its name from the Latin "octo" which means "eight" even after the months January and February were inserted into the calendar that was originally created by the Romans.

Herb of the Month:	Calendula
Candle Color:	Orange
Seventh Holy Stone:	Chrysoprase
Birthstone Pendulum:	Opal

Day 1
 All of my roads lead to happiness, love, balance and success!

Day 2

> *Today I claim all my dreams, my wants, my needs and my success! They are gifted to me by the universe.*

Day 3

> *Today I give myself permission to reach for my dreams and total success!*

Day 4

> *Today I refuse to be held back by my own fear and self-pity; I claim the power I need to move forward!*

Day 5

> *I refuse to give up until I have tried every avenue to my success!*

Day 6

> *Today I choose to push forward because giving up would be too easy!*

Day 7

> *Today I decide it's time to go big or go home; I choose to go big and reach for all my dreams!*

Day 8

> *Today I tear down the walls around my heart and open my arms to accept love!*

Day 9

> *Today I let my lite shine brightly all the way to success!*

Day 10

> *Today I forgive those who have hurt me and move forward to happiness!*

Day 11

Today I am the captain of my own ship; I decide where my future lies!

Day 12

Today I give myself permission to dream big, fear not, and to walk in my own shining light!

Day 13

Today I give myself permission to love big, be happy, and to live well!

Day 14

Today I choose to take time to enjoy my life and my success!

Day 15

Today I give myself permission to put me first!

Day 16

My life is full of possibilities; it's my decision which ones I make happen!

Day 17

Today I have the courage to follow my dreams and the knowledge to make them happen!

Day 18

I release the fear that's holding me back and I give myself permission to be happy!

Day 19

Today I choose persistence over power; persistence can cut through a mountain!

Day 20

Today I'm content with what I have; tomorrow will bring me what I want!

Day 21

Today I looked within myself for the answers; I look with an open mind and a open-heart.

Day 22

Today I except change; without change I cannot move forward to follow my dreams!

Day 23

I refuse to be a prisoner of the past; today I cut those ties that binds me!

Day 24

Today I choose to be strong, brave and humble in the shadows of weakness, fear and victory!

Day 25

Today I rejoice in the power to remove all obstacles out of my way to my happiness!

Day 26

Today I rolled over the Humps and crashed through the roadblocks; nothing can stop me from my success!

Day 27

Today I am not only wishing for my dreams to come true; I'm on the road to make my dreams happen!

Day 28

If you don't move towards your dreams they will evaporate like smoke on the wind!

Day 29

Today I choose to walk forward towards my dreams instead of walking backwards into the past!

Day 30

Today I stopped talking about my dreams and take action to make them happen!

Day 31

Today I leave the past in the dark and I move forward into the light of day and into my dreams!

Month of November

Trivia: This is the beginning of the festival for the Ancestors.

Herb of the Month:	Chrysanthemum
Candle Color:	Red
Seventh Holy Stone:	Jacinth
Birthstone Pendulum:	Topaz

Day 1

Today I see how wonderful and loved I am!
I give myself permission to be all I can be!

Day 2

Remember as the storm clouds brew that the sun will soon shine!

Day 3

I refuse to be held back by others' expectations of me; the only thing that counts is what I expect of myself!

Day 4

Today I take off the mask the world has placed on me and I become MY true self!

Day 5

You hold the key to your happiness; unlock the door and walk through it!

Day 6

Today I move forward with less talk and more action!

Day 7

Today I stop talking about my dreams and take the steps to make them happen!

Day 8

Today I stop waiting for someone else to make my dreams happen; I take full responsibility in making them happen!

Day 9

Today I surround myself with those things that will make my dreams come true.

Day 10

We are what we think! In order to be successful you have to think success!

Day 11

May I see myself as I want the world to see me!

Day 12

Happiness starts from the inside then flows outward; it can lead you to great things!

Day 13

You can't change the world but you can change yourself one thought at a time!

Day 14

Your life is your novel; you can rewrite the chapters if you want too!

Day 15

Your happiness begins and ends with you; gas up and move forward!

Day 16

Don't let fear drive you! Take over the driver's seat and head towards your dreams!

Day 17

Today I see my life as a gift! I'm unwrapping it and taking it out of the BOX!

Day 18

Today accept that you are your own extraordinary gift to the world!

Day 19

STOP! Fear is like a fungus; the more you water it the more it grows!

Day 20

Today I take off the blinders and see myself as the wonderful gifted person I am!

Day 21

Today I let go of my past so I can move forward into my future!

Day 22

Today I have faith that all my dreams will come true as long as I move forward into them!

Day 23

Today I make a stand when things get tough; I WILL stand strong and work through it!

Day 24

Remember your accomplishments are someone else's prayers waiting to be answered! Today I choose to Be GRATFUL!

Day 25

Today I choose to look at my past as a learning experience; not a mistake I made!

Day 26

If you wallow in what you don't have; then how will you achieve your goals?

Day 27

Today I choose to take a small step out of my box to reach for my dreams!

Day 28

I'm making my dreams happen one small step at the time!

Day 29

Today I choose to let my past to be just that — my past; I refuse to let it over shadow my life!

Day 30

Today I choose to step away from my fears and limitations I set for myself; I'm stepping out of the box!

MONTH OF DECEMBER

Trivia: Santa Claus is associated with Saint Nicholas..

Herb of the Month: Holly
Candle Color: Red and White
Seventh Holy Stone: Amethyst
Birthstone Pendulum: Turquoise

Day 1

Today I choose to see folks as they really are; not how I want them to be!

Day 2

Today I choose to change the way I think; instead of saying I can't; I KNOW I can!

Day 3

Today I choose to see what a magnificent and caring person I am!

Day 4

My potential is unlimited! I radiate love, honor and success!

Day 5

I am dressed with prosperity and abundance! My life is overflowing with love honor and success!

Day 6

I walk to my own tune of abundance, prosperity, love and success!

Day 7

I radiate with prosperity, success and love!

Day 8

I choose to let the past go as I move forward into my future!

Day 9

I refuse to sit around and wait for my dreams to happen; today I make them happen!

Day 10

I refuse to let my flaws hinder me; they are perfection in the making!

Day 11

For every failure success is on the horizon!

Day 12

Today I take the trash out and with it jealousy, envy, and hate of my haters!

Day 13

The more my haters hate the harder I will push to prove them wrong!

Day 14

I move forward down the highway towards SUCCESS!

Day 15

There is no wrong way for me to travel; all my roads lead to unlimited success!

Day 16

I walk in the light of self-confidence and abundance!

Day 17

I refuse to take on others' limitations; I move freely towards my goals!

Day 18

Today I refuse to be fenced in and boxed up; I'm breaking free to follow my dreams!

Day 19

Today I STOP making wishes and START making my dreams come true!

Day 20

Today I give myself permission to make my dreams a reality!

Day 21

I reaching for the stars but I'll take the moon!

Day 22

I take a stand! My little light may go dim but it will never go out!

Day 23

Tomorrow never comes so today I move forward towards my goals!

Day 24

Today I stop taking the easy way out by being miserable; I'll do the work to find happiness!

Day 25

Today I push the door to abundance and success open; I choose to walk through it!

Day 26

The only goal that is out of reach is the one I'm too lazy to reach for!

Day 27

Making plans is easy; following through with them takes work!

Day 28

Today I choose to be the best that I can be!

Day 29

Today I run over all obstacles in the way of my dreams!

Day 30

If you're on the road to success there's no time to go into reverse!

Day 31

Today I let go of the old to make room for the NEW!

REMEDIES

I wanted to add a few remedies that I grew up with. I am not suggesting that anyone try them by any means. If you do then you take full responsibility for any adverse effects.

When we were children we never went to the doctor my Mama treated us.

For Bruising and Cramps
> *Mama would rub the area with "sweet oil" then apply a warm cloth. This worked really well for cramps.*

To Cure a Cough
> *A table spoon of sugar and a drop of Kerosene.*
> *A large swallow of Vicks Salve*

For Congestion

> A pot of water boiling on the stove with Vicks Salve added to the water.

> Mama would make a Mustard plaster and make us lay with it on our chest. You have to be careful and not put it directly on the skin because it will burn.

Rashes

> She would either dust us with Talc or with corn starch.

Head lice or dry scalp

> Sassafras oil was applied to our scalps then wrapped in a white towel; then washed out in about 4 hours.

Ear Ache

> Four garlic cloves that have been steeped in Olive Oil. Warm and add a few drops to the ear.

Hot Toddy

> This was my Daddy's remedy and I wanted to add it. He kept a bottle of this made up and if we got sick we got a dose and had to go to bed.

> > 2 peppermint candies
> > Half of squeezed lemon
> > A gulp of Honey
> > A shot glass of whiskey

> He would heat it up and we had to drink it. There was no money to go to the doctor.

Boils and other Sores

If one of us got a boil Mama would put a piece of fat meat between gauze and tape it to us. I don't know how it worked but it would draw out the infection.

Bee Stings

If we got stung mama would put tobacco on it to draw out the poison.

Tooth Ache

If any of us got a tooth ache mama would wrap a few cloves up in a white handkerchief and make up hold it next to the infected tooth. You have to be careful because cloves will burn.

Diaper rash

Used bacon grease rubbed on the afflicted area to help with most diaper rashes.

Bottles

If you have a baby who just doesn't want to let go of their bottle then you can take them outside with their bottle and let them help you dig a hole. Drop the bottle in the hole and then y'all cover it up together. Tell them the bottle is gone. They may go looking for it a few times but they won't asked for it.

Nightmares

If you have a problem with nightmares you can place a sifter under your bed to sift them away while you sleep.

Bothersome Spirits

Sulphur in every corner will drive a bothersome spirit out of the house. A broom across the door way will keep them from entering.

I hope you have enjoyed these little tid bits from my childhood.

Be Blessed and be Happy!

RESOURCES

Starr Casas

    OldStyleConjure.com

    OldStyleConjure.BlogSpot.com

    BlogTalkRadio.com/OldStyleConjure

    Etsy.com/Shop/OldStyleConjure

Peter Paddon

    PendraigPublishing.com

The Serpent's Kiss

    Host of Conjure Con in Santa Cruz, Ca. is
a valuable resource for quality hand crafted
Conjure supplies. They even make their
own Florida water and candles! For more
information on events and products, visit
www.serpents-kiss.com

Orion Foxwood
    OrionFoxwood.com
Shimmering Wolf
    ShimmeringWolf.com
Sindy Todo
    TodoMojo.com
Conjure Crossroads
    FolkMagicFestival.com

About the Author

Starr Casas

I am an ol' Kentucky-born traditional Old Style Conjure woman who works with herbs, roots, and the Spirits. I am also known as a two headed root doctor and spiritual advisor. I learned how to do this work from my momma and grandmomma, who in turn, learned from their elders. Apart from my elders, I had wonderful folks coming into my life, who taught me hands on spiritual work.

Conjure, or what people now call Hoodoo, has always been around. In my family we didn't call it Hoodoo. We simply knew this to be "Conjure" or "work."

I have been a Conjure woman for over 50 years. I first learned how to read playing cards at 16, and by the time I was 17, I was already doing spiritual cleansings, or what some call uncrossing work, as well as healing work. At first I limited my work to the family, but when I turned 25, I knew it was time to start helping others. I began to do Conjure work full time for folks that were referred to me by my relatives or by others who knew me. I always worked only by word of mouth until three years ago, when I felt it was time to share my gift of Conjure work on the Internet.

I serve my community at my little shop where I offer consultations for those seeking help from a caring and compassionate spiritual worker. I also offer candle burning services to set a vigil light on troubles and concerns. I offer Conjure mini courses, as well as Old Style Conjure Oils, Conjure hands (mojo bags), Hoodoo prayer kits, Conjure bottles, and Conjure dollies to give power and domination. All of my products are blessed and prayed over by me to give clients the upper hand in all situations, to master their troubles and come out victorious, to be the leader that God wants them to be.

You can contact me at:

Website:
   OldStyleConjure.com

Email:
   Starr@OldStyleConjure.com

Blog:
   OldStyleConjure.blogspot.com

Blog Talk Radio:
   BlogTalkRadio.com/OldStyleConjure

OTHER BOOKS BY STARR CASAS

OLD STYLE CONJURE WORKBOOK
Volume I
WORKING THE ROOT

READING WITH OLD STYLE CONJURE CARDS

Available through:

PENDRAIG
Publishing

ALSO BY STARR CASAS

Hoodoo Money Conjure (revised)
Old Style Spiritual Cleansing
Old Style Conjure Book
Old Style Conjure Candle Burning
Working with Blackhawk
Working with the Bible

Magickal Works from Pendraig Publishing

Radomir Ristic
Balkan Traditional Witchcraft

Raymond Buckland
Buckland's Domino Divinaton
*Fortune-Telling with Döminös
and the Games of Döminös*

Buckland's Practical Color Magick

Eric De Vries
Hedge-Rider
Witches and the Underworld

Ed Fitch
Magical Rites from the Crystal Well
The Classic Book for Witches and Pagans

Veronica Cummer
Masks of the Muse
*Building a relationship
with the Goddess of the West*

Sorgitzak: Old Forest Craft
*Stories and messages
from the gods of Old Europe*

Dancing the Blood
Sorgitzak II

To Fly By Night
An Anthology of Hedgewitchery

Starr Casas
The Conjure Workbook
Vol I Working the Root

Reading with Old Style Conjure Cards
Vol I Working the Root Scott Stenwick

Mastering the Mystical Heptarchy
Vol I of the Mastering Enochian Magick Series

Ellen Evert Hopman
Scottish Herbs and Fairy Lore

Peter Paddon
Enchantment
*The Witch's Art of Manipulation by
Gesture, Gaze and Glamour*

Visceral Magick
*Bridging the Gap
Between Magic and Mundane*

A Grimoire for Modern Cunningfolk
*A Practical Guide to Witchcraft
on the Crooked Path*

The Crooked Path
*Selected Transcripts from
the Crooked Path Podcast*

Robin Artisson
The Flaming Circle
*A Reconstruction of the
Old Ways of Britain and Ireland*

The Horn of Evenwood

The Resurrection of the Meadow

Witching Way of the Hollow Hill
*The Gramarye of the Folk
Who Dwell Below the Mound*

Ann Finnin
The Forge of Tubal Cain
*Southern California Witchcraft,
Roebuck, and the Clan of Tubal Cain*

Fiction Novels from Pendraig Publishing

The Demon's Apprentice Series
by Ben Reeder

The Demon's Apprentice *Book 1*
The Page of Swords *Book II*

The Qaa Mysteries
by Claudia Dillaire

The Wrath of Amun *Book 1*
The Talisman of Tehuti *Book II*

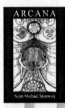

Arcana
by Scott Stenwick

The Tale of Tyrfing
by Sokarjo Stormwillow

Golden Illuminati
by Raymond Buckland

The 13th Moon
by Ilana Sturm

The Glastonbury Chronicles
by S.P. Hendrick

Uneasy Lies the Head *Volume I*

The Sword of the King *Volume II*

Coin of the Realm *Volume III*

The Rose Above the Sword *Volume IV*

The Blood of Kings *Volume V*

The Barley and the Rose *Volume VI*

Tales of the Dearg-Sidhe
by S.P. Hendrick

Son of Air and Darkness *Volume I*

Great Queen's Hound *Volume II*

The Pale Mare's Fosterling *Volume III*

CPSIA information can be obtained at www.ICGtesting.com
Printed in the USA
LVOW11s0132040615

441050LV00001B/24/P